THE
WALK

GORDON BOSTIC

Primix Publishing
East Brunswick Office Evolution
1 Tower Center Boulevard, Ste 1510
East Brunswick, NJ 08816
www.primixpublishing.com
Phone: 1-800-538-5788

Published by Primix Publishing: 10/24/2024

ISBN: 979-8-88703-414-0(sc)
ISBN: 979-8-88703-415-7(e)

Library of Congress Control Number: 2024917438

PRIMIX
PUBLISHING
THE WRITE CHOICE

Contents

Prolog

He had been judged a criminal
And sentenced to the Walk.
Though his attorneys filed appeals
The judge refused to balk.

He'd criticized the government
And for that he must pay.
His trial was nothing more than sham
To make him go away.

His lawyers thought the judgment harsh
But found their hands were tied.
For now, it's of no consequence
To find the witness lied.

The judge had granted him some time
To settle his affairs.
For once the Walk was underway
He would have other cares.

His family became distraught
When they had heard the news.
For they believed him innocent
As justice they'd abuse.

The Walk

The Walk was the alternative
To lengthy prison stays.
As a means to offer penance
For all their wicked ways.

Believed to be more civilized
Than locking them away.
As all who're judged as criminals
Would more humanely pay.

And there were financial savings
With prisons not required.
All they'd need was a walking course
That's easily acquired.

Though the punishment effective
For none would dare repeat
All the rigors of the journey
Once the Walk was complete.

He saw a woman in high heels
Who, clearly, had no clue
As to the purpose of the Walk
And what they're meant to do.

The Rules

The Walk was governed by few rules
But they were crystal clear.
And for any violation
The punishment severe.

Their course had been laid out for them
Which they were not to leave.
For any who abandoned it
Their family would greave.

And they'd not allow for stragglers
Who could not keep the pace.
For anyone who fell behind
Would be shot in the face.

They'd rest at night and twice a day
Where also they'd be fed.
But there're no accommodation
For where they'd make their bed.

A pardon would be granted those
Who made it to the end.
But history had proven that
It's not a likely trend.

The Start

There were twelve hundred at the start
And spirits had been high.
For most of them had been convinced
That few of them would die.

They gathered from all walks of life
As to the Walk subject.
While given no indication
Of what they could expect.

Their families surrounded them
Before the Walk began.
For most, it was to say goodbye
And hold them while they can.

The guards were called their chaperones
Though all had been well armed.
They were provided vehicles
And easily alarmed.

Though most proclaimed their innocence
There're none who truly cared.
Their chaperones unfeeling brutes
Who looked at them and glared.

All devices were collected
As they were not allowed.
The Walk was meant as punishment
Thus, they were disavowed.

Gordon Bostic

The One in Charge

A man called Belmont was in charge
Who showed no empathy.
It's rumored that he'd done the Walk
But had no sympathy.

His mission to enforce the rules
And maintain discipline.
Disturbing was his legacy
Wherever he had been.

They said that he'd been special trained
Specific for this task.
Though what had been the rationale
There're none who'd dare to ask.

Though most had been afraid of him
They thought, what could he do
With media so close at hand
And ev'rything in view.

That's when they found the media
Had from the Walk been banned.
Which had meant they're at the mercy
Of what he may demand.

The Chaperones

Their chaperones were none too kind
In fact, they'd proven cruel.
Compassion was unknown to them
As was the Golden Rule.

Most doubted they were citizens
But thought them guns for hire.
They could have shown civility
But proved they'd no desire.

Though language was a barrier
It's rare they'd even speak.
They had seemed morally challenged
As justice they'd not seek.

He found it very curious
They were to chaperone.
They looked more like a black ops team
Who were left on their own.

The Protester

Mark Jackson was a homeless vet
Who served until retired.
But when his service was complete
Found benefits expired.

The government had promised Mark
What it could not provide.
For all the money it would cost
Had not been set aside.

There was no future planning done
Except where it's concerned.
The money it skimmed from the top
As though it had been earned.

He moaned to representatives
That this had been unfair.
But their only explanation
The funds simply weren't there.

He took his protest to the street
So ev'ry one would know
The lies and empty promises
He had to undergo.

The Walk he knew was televised
And also drew a crowd.
He moved his protest to the start
Where he became quite loud.

Then declared a public nuisance.
Arrested on the spot.
He was subsequently ordered
To fill an empty slot.

He believed he'd been mistreated
Despite its fancy talk.
The government had lied to him
And now he had to walk.

All the Faces

As he studied all the faces
There're some he thought he knew.
Perhaps they're old acquaintances
Whose names he had no clue.

Like him they all appeared concerned
With what should happen next.
They'd all heard stories of the Walk
Which still left them perplexed.

It's said there could be accidents
That sometimes did occur.
But that had been unusual
That most would not endure.

Although they had assurances
There's no need for concern.
The glances that were passed around
Had left him with heartburn.

Day One

Day one had seemed a Sunday stroll
As they had walked en masse.
There were jokes and conversations
Although it had seemed crass.

They only were allowed three stops
So, if nature should call
They had been forced to soil themselves
Or not to walk at all.

Though to not walk was no option
As to where stopping led.
For those who would refuse to walk
Would be shot in the head.

The people who walked next to him
Were who he got to know.
Although they changed from day to day
With the Walk's ebb and flow.

They walked as if it's Madi Gras
And they're in the parade.
With the journey showing promise
Of new friends being made.

Gordon Bostic

The Car Salesman

Max Baker was a car salesman
And grossly overweight.
Five people claimed he cheated them
So, this became his fate.

He'd struggled to keep up with them
Right from the very start.
And those around him were concerned
How strong may be his heart.

He claimed his customers had lied
Because they were upset
They could have made a better deal
Were expectations met.

And thus, the cops charged him with fraud
Which he thought was not true.
For he merely was a salesman
Who did what salesmen do.

Dark Design

The media had been a part
Of ev'ry Walk before
But from this Walk they had been banned
Though none had known what for.

The government had its secrets
That it would not reveal.
The Walk had other purposes
That it chose to conceal.

Besides the common criminals
Were also dissidents
Who spoke against the government
Expressing their dissents.

The Walk gave opportunity
To quash rebellious lies.
Wherein each could be convicted
And sentenced as if spies.

It seemed the lack of media
Had been an evil sign.
This Walk was not the usual
But of a dark design.

The Priest

The priest was an anomaly
As they were rarely caught.
The charge was he molested boys
And then their silence bought.

But there're two who had stepped forward
To name him as accused.
They claimed he'd had his way with them
And they had been abused.

The priest had claimed it was a lie
But there were none to hear.
The crime incensed the neighborhood
And ended his career.

The judge had found he'd little choice
In how he had to rule.
The priest was sentenced to the Walk
As he had been old school.

The boys then chuckled to themselves
To see how it played out.
The only crime committed was
What they had been about.

Maryann

He felt someone starring at him
Which made him ill at ease.
When he looked down to see her there
With a smile meant to please.

She said her name was Maryann
And thought that he should know
Whatever path he chose to take
Was where she meant to go.

Though Maryann appeared fifteen
She had to be of age.
For minors weren't allowed to walk.
Instead, they had been caged.

Her mother said to stay with him
As she had known his wife.
For she knew he would protect her
And, maybe, save her life.

Truman

They all thought Truman was insane
But he just played the fool.
For all its secrets he had known
As he had been its tool.

Once darling of the government
Involved in its intrigue.
His missions always classified
And rumored major-league.

The government had always known
That Truman was a threat.
So, evidence it falsified
Where it could hedge its bet.

Thus, Truman had been made to walk
As it was evident
The Walk was clearly dangerous
And prone to accident.

A Sense of Faith

He'd never had a sense of faith
For he'd not seen the need.
As those he'd seen profess a faith
Still wallowed in their greed.

He saw the pure hypocrisy
That, clearly, they displayed.
With claims of things that they believed
Too easily waylaid.

They claimed that there were promises
Of what they would receive.
But he questioned by their actions
If they'd truly believe.

He almost wished faith he possessed
In lieu of what he faced.
For once the Walk truly began
Their faith would be replaced.

Gordon Bostic

The Innocent

Brianne had seemed so innocent
He could not figure why
She had been sentenced to the Walk
Where she'd most likely die.

She was convicted of a crime
That she did not commit.
Her lawyer was a worthless fool
But that's not half of it.

He wanted her to sleep with him
But when she had refused
The jerk rejected a plea deal.
Where she would be excused.

She tried explaining to the judge
But he refused to hear.
So, he, in spite, had sentenced her
And that's why she was here.

The Advocate

Melinda was an advocate
The government despised.
For she'd point out injustices
It thought it had disguised.

She had known its interworking
And secrets it had kept.
She'd proven she was resolute
As if she never slept.

She's a clear and present danger
With whom it had to deal.
So, it falsified some charges
As she refused to kneel.

The one witness it would present
Summarily had lied.
And those who'd choose to contradict
Suspiciously, had died.

Then when the verdict had been read
She saw what had occurred.
Because she was a threat to it
True justice had been blurred.

The Noontime Break

The noontime break was a relief
As he was tired and sore.
Though Maryann had looked refreshed
And could have walked some more.

A sandwich was provided each
Comprised of Spam and cheese.
Though some had viewed it with disgust,
Hunger it did appease.

The tenor of the Walk had changed
The further that they went.
It's no longer an excursion
Where time with friends was spent.

They still had hours yet to walk
Before, again, they'd rest.
From here on out each step they took
It's their resolve they'd test.

Then Maryann had helped him up
As he was stiff and sore.
For they were ordered to resume
And walk the Walk once more.

John Lambert

He despised that kid, John Lambert,
Who hit on Maryann.
Though she paid him no attention,
He looked to have a plan.

He'd warned him once to stay away
Which Lambert had ignored.
So, the next time he approached her
It's Lambert that he floored.

Though his wife and he were childless
They still had maintained hope
That one day they may still be blessed.
Till then, they had to cope.

But now that he found Maryann
He had felt like a dad.
So, it's Lambert's clear intentions
That really made him mad.

Gordon Bostic

The Course

Maryann asked what had bothered him
As he seemed lost in thought.
He said the course had puzzled him
As answers he'd not bought.

The course was like an interstate
Except there were no lines.
Below its shoulders were plain fields
Devoid of brush and vines.

The tree line sat back fifty yards
And that's on either side.
If someone dared to try escape
There was no place to hide.

Most thought it also curious
There were no barriers.
As though it's an invitation
To become harriers.

The Call Girl

Debbie Lynn had been a temptress
Who always was on-call.
A fav'rite of the government
Until she took the fall.

She served the highest echelon
And always was discrete.
She clearly knew the jeopardy
If she should fail to meet.

She always thought she was secure
As she they would protect.
But it was false security
With what she knew suspect.

Too many secrets she had known
Derived from pillow talk.
Although she promised not to tell
She still was made to walk.

The Architect

Fred Thompson was an architect
Whose building had collapsed.
He thought that he was powerful
But found his power lapsed.

He claimed it was construction crews
Who were responsible.
It's true that they were his designs
Which they found plausible.

It seemed the crews had bought the judge
With how the ruling read.
The crews had followed his designs
Exactly as he said.

But since the crews used his designs
The fault laid not with them.
For it seemed his plans were faulty
Which placed the blame on him.

He noticed Fred had a slight limp
Which he had pointed out.
But Fred claimed that it was nothing
He should worry about.

The Secrets

He could see it in their faces.
The secrets they'd conceal.
Those past misdeeds or evil thoughts
That they cannot repeal.

It seemed each person on the Walk
Had secrets they wished hid.
But as the Walk dragged on and on
Those secrets they'd be rid.

As each had grown more desperate
Confessions would be made.
As none would surely wish to die
With sins that went unpaid.

What good were secrets anyway
To those already dead.
The Walk was more than punishment
As on their souls it fed.

Gordon Bostic

The Accountant

James Reacher was an accountant
Who served the government.
Who had found a discrepancy
In what it said it spent.

But when he brought the fact to light
He found to his dismay
The government had been aware
But had nothing to say.

Instead, it charged him with a crime
And claimed embezzlement.
The court had then upheld the charge
On a flawed argument.

Then he was sentenced by the book
Although it was not fair.
For he was not the criminal
But no one seemed to care.

That Night

That night when they had stopped to rest
She sat down next to him.
Maryann claimed they were a team
Against the rest of them.

She felt the longer that they walked
The danger would increase
With patience slowly worn away
Their morals would decrease.

Her eyes would sparkle when she spoke
For comfort she had found.
She felt her safety was assured
As long as he's around.

He stood on watch as she laid down
And drifted off to sleep.
For he felt an obligation
He swore that he would keep.

Gordon Bostic

Day Two

Day two he woke with Maryann
All curled up by his side.
It appeared she'd not been lying
That with him she'd abide.

He gently woke her to the day
And helped her to prepare.
As ev'ryone resumed the Walk
Without any fanfare.

He thought it wiser to remain
Towards middle of the pack.
There was no need to be in front
And, surely, not in back.

He watched the fools who rushed ahead
As though it was a race.
For he thought it was more prudent
To set a steady pace.

Belmont's Address

The rules were now in his domain
And he wished to be clear
That they will do as they were told
Or their Walk ended here.

He had no qualms nor misgivings
To do what must be done.
For they were here for punishment
And it would not be fun.

Whatever dreams they may have had
Should all be placed on hold.
He meant to make this punishment
To be both harsh and cold.

For they were proven criminals
Who had a debt to pay
And his instructions had been clear
There was no other way.

So, any effort to escape
Would be futile at best.
Thus, any thoughts or plans they've made
They should not wish to test.

A Motley Crew

They truly were a motley crew
Of noted miscreants.
They ranged from hardened criminals
To lowly malcontents.

Their only commonality
Was here they were assigned.
The Walk was theirs to undertake
And to that were resigned.

The Walk did not play favorites
But treated all the same.
Regardless of their lot in life
Or of their claim to fame.

For they're now a band of brothers
Upon a common quest.
Where neither guilt nor innocence
Were measures of the test.

The Master of Their Fate

Belmont reviewed them as they passed
As if they're on parade.
As if he was a general
Their sacrifices made.

He studied them with pure disdain
Assessing who's a threat.
For some of them, he had been told,
Had fates already set.

He was the master of their fate
For their lives he'd now own.
Until the Walk had been complete
And misdeeds they'd atone.

He thought they were a sorry lot
Who'd been placed in his charge.
But he had justice to dispense
And orders to discharge.

Gordon Bostic

The Death of the Priest

The priest it seemed had passed away
In silence of the night.
His guilt, guards claimed, had taken him
To that eternal light.

But they had no explanation
For the state he was in.
The commission of suicide
Had been a mortal sin.

So, there had been many doubters
That what they're told untrue.
For suicide was not something
A priest would ever do.

Though the guards were quite adamant
To what it was they found.
A fact the guards would not release,
His hands and feet were bound.

The Associate

Annette had given ev'rything
But found she was betrayed.
She worked within the government
But found she had been played.

For she was an associate
Who did as she was told.
But those to whom she'd answer to
Were deceitful and cold.

Annette had known the hidden facts
They had not wished revealed.
Surprisingly, she got this far
And life not yet repealed.

Although she thought her loyalty
Was all they would demand.
When there came investigations
Her sacrifice they'd planned.

She disputed the evidence
But all to no avail.
Too late she saw the fix was in
And she was bound for hell.

The Damaged Vet

Rick Blackledge was a veteran
Who came home damaged goods.
And found the things it promised him
Had been blatant falsehoods.

He complained treatments promised him
He never had received.
When he swore he would go public
The government grew peeved.

Rick then had written articles
Denouncing what they did.
Which to it was an annoyance
Of which it would be rid.

With judgment coming very swift
For those who'd rock the boat.
The Walk the sentence he received
Because of what he wrote.

How it all Began

When Maryann had asked him if
He knew how it began.
The question caught him by surprise
As though that was her plan.

He mulled it over for a while
Before he dared to speak.
He wanted to be accurate
But not overly bleak.

The government had run amok
So great had been its greed.
The taxes that it had imposed
Had never met its need.

But there were none to specify
To where the money went.
As soon as taxes had rolled in
The money had been spent.

So, it had levied penalties
For those who would not pay.
But ran out of facilities
Where they'd be locked away.

Yet to build new facilities
Would bear a heavy cost
And funds were not available
Due to how much it lost.

Gordon Bostic

For money it would allocate
Would simply disappear.
Which really did not matter as
A new tax would appear.

The Walk a good alternative
To prison time received.
With no need for facilities
And punishment achieved.

The populace it did persuade
The Walk was more humane
Than years and years of prison time
With costs that were insane.

Expanded then to punish those
Convicted of a crime.
Incarceration then was banned
As just a waste of time.

The Walk began as punishment
For those who did not pay
The taxes that the government
Had dared upon them lay.

The Walk the final arbiter
Of guilt or innocence.
The populace was sold on that
Although it made no sense.

The Psychopath

Nick Russell was a psychopath
Who all had left alone.
He bragged he killed so many men
A graveyard he could own.

He demonstrated no remorse
For anything he'd done.
In fact, he seemed to relish it
As fame it seemed he won.

The guards treated him with caution
Believing him a threat.
Though others gladly they'd abuse
It's Nick they'd not upset.

It's as though they had admired him.
Perhaps for what he did.
As each of them would do the same
But they'd go off the grid.

The walk for him was justified
And something well deserved.
The only case that he had seen
Where justice had been served.

Gordon Bostic

The Homeless Woman

Nicole had been left destitute
After her husband died.
For he had run up gambling debts
That he'd always denied.

The court ordered restitution
Then sold all that she had.
The result had left her homeless
And hunger drove her mad.

It was a piece of fruit she stole
Which led to her arrest.
And since she had been indigent
There're none who could attest.

And now she walked the same as they
Accepting of her fate.
From grace she fell to poverty
And life was not that great.

The Prostitute

Michelle had been a prostitute
So, habit she could feed.
Her body was the thing she sold
To get what she had need.

They'd busted her so many times
Police knew her by name.
The judge had thrown the book at her.
Pervasive was his claim.

She had granted many favors
To keep herself from jail.
But one day that caught up to her
And they'd refused her bail.

Solicitation was the charge
Which served to land her here.
And while her habit went unfed
Her mind was less than clear.

The Old Man

The old man still ran marathons
But this was not the same.
He sometimes slowed his pace to chat
But he'd not known his name.

He spoke against the government
For which he had been tried.
They quickly had convicted him
As witnesses had lied.

The old man kept a steady pace
Though he was elderly.
Although he had no wish to die
It seemed a certainty.

But judgment was already passed
With nothing he could do.
Except rely upon his faith
Somehow, he'd see this through.

The Victim

Young Sarah had been victimized
By one of high esteem.
One of the highest echelon
Who did as he would deem.

She went to the authorities
With charge to the event.
Although it seemed she was ignored
Was pretty evident.

Frustration ate away at her
To where her anger grew.
The bastard had his way with her
And lots of people knew.

Then she dared a confrontation
To get into his face.
The man's a proven reprobate
Who was a true disgrace.

He laughed at her as he pushed through
With ev'ry confidence
That she had simply been a fool
Who lacked the evidence.

Surprisingly, he had looked shocked
When he had seen the gun.
The trigger she pulled only once
And his life had been done.

Gordon Bostic

Her trial was pretty cut and dry
As it was all on tape.
Although she claimed the man she killed
Assaulted her with rape.

The judge had said, if that were true
She could have filed a charge.
Instead, she took it on herself
With vengeance to discharge.

The jury was not out for long
As they refused to balk.
The judge then claimed he had no choice.
So, sentence was to walk.

The Whistleblower

They called Miranda a psychic
As there were things she knew.
Like secrets that the government
Had wished no one to view.

She'd circumvent its policies
Although it knew not how.
It seemed it found no evidence
So, guilt she'd disavow.

It had no proof of anything
Yet, secrets she released.
A whistleblower by design
With secrets she had fleeced.

It had to put a stop to it
Before real damage done.
Miranda, thus, the principal
In the charge that was spun.

It claimed she was a foreign spy
Where she had no defense.
So, she was sentenced to the walk
To pay for her offense.

Gordon Bostic

The Graduate

Ann was a recent graduate
With loans she could not pay.
Although she had earned her degree
No job had come her way.

The court had found her in arrears
And, thus, committed fraud.
For she'd accepted all the loans
They claimed so to defraud.

Though her conviction was suspect
As thousands did the same.
Her knowledge of their policies
Could prove that they were lame..

So, she was sentenced to the Walk
With hope she would expire.
As she had a heart condition
At birth she did acquire.

Fred's Return

The next day they again saw Fred
Whose limp was more pronounced.
It seemed he was in agony
Though it went unannounced.

His shoes were not appropriate
For what he'd undergone.
His feet were blistered to extreme
As soles were nearly gone.

He noticed Fred left tracks of blood
And struggled to keep pace.
He saw the panic in Fred's eyes
With fear what he may face.

He knew he could not carry him
So not sure what to do.
His heart truly went out to Fred
And what he had been through.

But as the day wore on and on
Poor Fred had dropped behind.
The gunshot caught them by surprise
And brought no peace of mind.

Gordon Bostic

The Terminal Man

Jack Nichols had been terminal
But sentenced anyway.
His lawyers filed many appeals
Yet none would grant a stay.

The government had filed a claim
Since he could not be saved.
It could revoke his benefits
And health care should be waived.

But Jack had caught it by surprise
And filed a countersuit.
That said it was obligated
And its claim had been moot.

Though Jack's suit had been rejected
As merit it had none.
The suit then ruled as frivolous
With Jack's life mostly done.

The Socialite

She was of high society
But one mistake she made.
Her wealth she would accumulate
But taxes had not paid.

She thought she was above the law
As wealth made her immune.
But when the government found out
It struck like a monsoon.

It confiscated all she had
Declaring it a fine.
And then, it had arrested her
For she had crossed the line.

She did the best that she could do
To keep her from the Walk.
But when it asked who aided her
She had refused to talk.

Gordon Bostic

Truman's Plan

There were devices they possessed
The guards were unaware.
For they were mostly hooligans
And thus, not tech aware.

So, data passed among the group
They labeled malcontents.
It's Truman who collected it
And guarded its contents.

But now that Truman was at risk
The data he must hide.
Though he could find no hiding spot
That they could not have spied.

The only one beyond reproach
Had guarded Maryann.
The data he would pass to him.
At least, that was his plan.

The Shot

The first time that they heard a shot
It came as a surprise.
The rumors then had quickly spread
Of Max Baker's demise.

The rumors were that he collapsed
As he was nearly dead.
The guards could not get him to stand
So, shot him in the head.

Of course, there was no evidence
As he was in the rear.
But now the mood of all had changed
For now, they walked in fear.

Then Maryann had grabbed his hand
As though that would assure
He would not let her fall behind
Nor would let go of her.

Gordon Bostic

The Second Night

The second night as they sat down
His legs began to cramp.
Though Maryann tried rubbing them
They'd no wish to unclamp.

She tried her best to comfort him
But all to no avail.
The pain had brought him close to tears
As he began to flail.

The others in proximity
Had merely sat and stared.
For now, their world was dog-eat-dog
Where no one really cared.

The pain, at last, seemed to subside
As he held Maryann.
For then he'd come to recognize
Devolvement now began.

The Mystery

Both nights when he laid down to sleep
He watched her bow her head.
Giving thanks to some deity
That she was not yet dead.

He'd never dared broach the subject
Not wishing her upset.
But he'd never found the solace
That she would seem to get.

He'd never been a man of faith
For he'd not seen the need.
Believing in some unseen force
Whose guidance he should heed.

He thought it was a fairy tale
Designed to serve the meek.
He'd never found the need for it
As he was not that weak.

Gordon Bostic

Dark Days

The dark days were ahead of them
Of that he had been sure.
And nothing good could come of it
With what they'd seen occur.

He noticed all the guards were armed
And medics, there were none.
Which had led to nervous feelings
That they're as good as done.

But Belmont was the greater threat
As he's the one in charge.
He had command of all their lives
With orders to discharge.

The thing that frightened him the most
Was what those orders were.
He wanted to see Beth again
But that may not occur.

Though he could not be positive
He can't ignore the dread
Of ev'rything that's yet to come
Meant dark days were ahead.

Day Three

Day three began with tragedy
To find the old man dead.
The rumors had been prevalent
That someone smashed his head.

But the Walk had still proceeded
As though nothing occurred.
There were suspicions that were raised
Where foul play was inferred.

But there had been no evidence
That anyone had seen.
They only had the words of guards
Whose records went unseen.

The Walk was now a drudgery
That none had wished to face.
The tears he saw that freely flowed
Were surely no disgrace.

A Change came over Them

At first, they were like family
Both helpful and concerned.
But as the miles dragged on and on
That feeling grossly turned.

Cooperation had been lost
As all wished to survive.
And sacrifices authorized
For those who'd stay alive.

It was now self-preservation
That was their main concern.
So, if a fellow walker fell
There're few of them who'd turn.

There was a tension that had grown
It seemed with ev'ry mile.
There was no more frivolity
And few had dared to smile.

Their Stories

All the walkers had a story
Each needed to be told.
For some to claim their innocence.
Some let their guilt unfold.

Some had sought to gain forgiveness
So saddled with remorse.
While some others looked for answers
To why they walked this course.

Some stories had been heartbreaking.
Some stories seemed a lie.
Some stories seemed to be made up
Though he could not say why.

Though their stories had been varied,
They're also much the same.
For all of them were judged guilty
With penalty the same.

Maryann's Story

To break the boredom of the Walk
He turned to Maryann
And asked her what it was she did
That brought her to this clan.

She had been with a group of friends
Who chose to dine and dash.
She stayed behind to make amends
But did not have the cash.

They told her they would let her go
If she'd give up the names.
But she refused to be a rat
So, she suffered the claims.

Council asked for leniency
The judge cruelly denied.
Although she had done nothing wrong
The truth had not applied.

He'd never been a Father

He had never been a father
Though Beth and he had tried.
Now Maryann had seemed the child
That they had been denied.

He felt a fondness for the girl
Though much he did not know.
She clearly put her faith in him.
That much she dared to show.

So now he felt responsible
Concerning her welfare.
As though a daughter he had found
Dependent on his care.

He made a promise to himself
As long as he'd survive.
He would do what's necessary
To keep the girl alive.

Gordon Bostic

The Runner

He heard someone behind him say
That he could take no more.
There was a world beyond the Walk
That he wished to explore.

The rest could walk themselves to death
But he had been too smart.
He'd closely watched their chaperones
And had been since the start.

He'd duly noted their routines
To catch them when off guard.
And he thought he'd found an opening
He could not disregard.

He tried to make a run for it
But failed in the attempt.
He barely had escaped the course
When shot in pure contempt.

The ruckus caused the Walk to stall
As all in horror starred.
The chaperones collected him
As if they had not cared.

Belmont's Philosophy

Belmont had one philosophy
That when mistakes were made
The one who was responsible
Would be the one who paid.

The guard had seen the walker run
But chose to do nothing.
Two other guards had shot him down
While he stood there watching.

Because he had been hesitant
Belmont became enraged.
He put his gun to the guard's head
And trigger had engaged.

He declared it an example
Of what may lie ahead.
If any who would try escape
Would next be rendered dead.

Gordon Bostic

The Body

They left the body where it fell
Where all who passed it by
Had wondered why a warning shot
They had not thought to try.

It was clear their lives were worthless
With the Walk underway.
His body was a warning sign
That those who could should pray.

They're nothing more than animals
The guards were hired to herd.
If some were lost along the way
It had not been unheard.

The hope that they had held onto
Had seemed to slip away.
As they stared upon the body
That by the course would lay.

The Encounter

When Truman moved up next to him
It's wary he became.
Truman was clearly targeted
And to the guards fair game.

He spoke against the government
And for that he was tried.
Conviction a formality
As ev'ry witness lied.

Truman said he knew his story
For his was much the same.
He criticized the government
Then he, it dared to frame.

Then he passed him a small thumb drive
He said had evidence
Documenting its corruption
And claims were pure nonsense.

Then Truman had dropped off the pace
And faded towards the rear.
He stuffed the drive into his pants
But did so with great fear.

Gordon Bostic

Monsters

She never believed in monsters
But now she knew they're real.
For they clearly walked among them
And with them they must deal.

No mercy had been shown to those
Who may not be at fault.
They executed each of them
As though by some default.

Then when the guards had been assured
That none remained alive.
They ordered those who still were left
To rise and Walk revive.

Dead bodies were strewn ev'rywhere
But no one seemed to care.
For once the Walk they had resumed
Not one had seen them there.

Her Faith

He noticed Maryann had prayed
Whenever she'd the chance.
At first, he had convinced himself
It had been happenstance.

He thought it was a waste of time
But he'd not intercede.
The act, though, seemed to comfort her
And that he must concede.

He saw how deeply she believed
And knew it was not fake.
Her faith had seemed to carry her
In ev'ry choice she'd make.

He marveled at her confidence
In what was wrong and right.
She had a set of principles
For which she's not contrite.

Though the things that she believed in
He mostly, too, believed.
Her faith it seemed was absolute
As peace she had achieved.

Gordon Bostic

Rumors of Informants

There were rumors of informants
Embedded in the Walk.
Who would spy on conversations
And eavesdrop on loose talk.

But the rumors raised suspicions
That haunted them with doubt.
Where anything they'd chance to say
The guards would soon find out.

It mattered not if they were true.
The damage had been done.
It made them individuals
Who now would trust no one.

For ev'ryone had grown guarded
And all trust had been lost.
But the rumors were effective
Though few cared what it cost.

The Third Night

The third night he broke down and cried
In light of what occurred.
So many lives were lost that day
With anger undeterred.

Resentment was a living thing
That neither side would hide.
As each had looked for an excuse
The other to blindside.

There'd grown such animosity
Where life became so cheap
Some walkers grew so paranoid
They were afraid to sleep.

For it seemed death trolled the darkness
As each morn they would hear
At least one walker passed away
Though reasons were not clear.

Gordon Bostic

Truman's Return

He was surprised Truman returned
Later that very night.
There's one thing more he must divulge
That should be brought to light.

Truman had whispered that her name
Was all he could reveal.
The information she required
Was what he must conceal.

The woman's name was Brandywine
But that was all he knew.
The thumb drive he had given him
Was who it should go to.

He had been grateful Maryann
Had slept through the affair.
He thought it safer she'd not known
That Truman had been there.

What Truman Left

It seemed that Truman left a note
To destroy after read.
The contents truly frightened him
Truman may soon be dead.

It said he was expendable
Because the truth he'd known.
There's no one else he could turn to
Whose trust was clearly shown.

He'd seen how he protected her
And faith she'd shown in him.
He was the only one he thought
Who'd not give in to them.

It said he knew they're watching him
And his time may be short.
So, if he saw him on the Walk
Contact he should abort.

Gordon Bostic

The Shadow Government

There was a shadow government
That somehow gained control.
Who thought they were untouchable
And, clearly, had no soul.

Elections now were frivolous
As they were so ingrained.
Regardless what the voters said
Their power was maintained.

That government had wished to cleanse
The world of its mistakes.
It acted with impunity
Despite how high the stakes.

It's not the government at large
That proved to be at fault.
Instead there was an element
Behind this cruel assault.

Day Four

The fourth day started with gunshots
As three to walk refused.
Two more were killed attacking guards.
Their actions unexcused.

Ev'ry day there had been rumors
A walker had been killed.
But now he'd seen the evidence
That left him feeling chilled.

A shiver had gone through the group
To find it's not a lie.
Two choices were available:
They'd either walk or die.

Each day sponsored more resentment
That this had been their fate.
The government was who they blamed
As fear had turned to hate.

Social Distancing

He noticed as the Walk progressed
How strung out they'd become.
He could not see the lead or end
Nor knew how far they'd come.

It seemed the rumors that were spread
Accomplished their intent.
As conversations had been short
And few said what they meant.

As though it's social distancing
In which they were engaged.
As people kept their distances
Afraid who they'd enraged.

With all fearing who's complicit
With Belmont and his thugs.
As there also had been rumors
They'd truth revealing drugs.

Lambert's Return

Jim Lambert had shown up again
With one thing on his mind.
He came up next to Maryann
As though she's hard to find.

Though his efforts to impress her
Had seemed a little lame.
He did draw out a smile from her
And got to know her name.

But acting as her protector
He chased Lambert away.
He did not like the boy that much
So, sent him on his way.

Though Lambert seemed to be annoyed
Jim left to move ahead.
He felt a certain sense of guilt
When they found he was dead.

Gordon Bostic

The Smell

The smell no longer bothered him
As they all smelled the same.
They had been stripped of dignity
Which was replaced with shame.

There were no showers nor fresh clothes,
No bathroom nor a sink.
The only water they supplied
Was just enough to drink.

They were not human any more
Though not quite animal.
They had been forced to see themselves
As less than minimal.

And all of them were left debased
With spirits broken too.
It's Belmont's job to crush their souls
Which he was glad to do.

The Paradox

He noticed as the Walk progressed
Some abnormalities.
As though agendas were in play
With obscure subtleties.

Some walkers had been ostracized
And singled for abuse.
As though they had been targeted
Though reasons were obtuse.

For there were individuals
They seemed to see as threat
And they were punished more severe
If their demands weren't met.

It seemed to be a paradox
Where all were meant to pay.
But there seemed to be exceptions
They went out of their way.

Death of the Psychopath

The psychopath the guards admired.
At least, that's how it seemed.
He got a pass for errors made
No other could redeem.

Until that day he turned on them
When two guards he had killed.
He'd confiscated cutlery
And urges had fulfilled.

One guard had shot him at point blank
But he refused to die.
The psychopath then turned on him
And stabbed him in the eye.

Next shots rang out in rapid fire
As though there was a war.
The psychopath it seemed was dead
When they shot him once more.

The Reports

Although the media was banned
They still received reports
Though the data had been filtered
By government escorts.

Thus, reports had been sanitized
But not enough to lie.
They merely failed to recognize
The who, the where and why.

For abuses were not mentioned
Nor was untimely death.
Reporting only progress made
Along with depth and breath.

Though what was cleared was factual
It left out one detail
Conditions were deplorable
Where life a living hell.

Gordon Bostic

The Altercation

An altercation had occurred
It seemed a guard invoked.
Whatever was the cause of it
The woman seemed provoked.

The ruckus caused the Walk to pause
As all had froze in place.
The guard pulled out a wood baton
And struck her 'cross her face.

In effort to defend herself
She lashed out at the guard.
She caught him with a lucky punch
To where he went down hard.

The guard recovered very fast
And clearly was not done.
His rage had taken hold of him
As he pulled out his gun.

The woman tried to get away
But from the course had strayed.
The bullets had ripped into her.
She now in silence laid.

Infections

The smell, at first, had made him gag
But slowly seemed to fade..
For he'd no longer notice it
Or sense of smell decayed.

Some women tried to clean themselves
While guards would laugh and jeer.
Then, suddenly, those efforts stopped
Embarrassed by their leer.

There were no medics to be found
And guards had never cared.
So, any tiny injury
Could easily have flared.

Infections, then, became the norm
From blisters that had bled.
The filth in which they're made to live
Would soon augment the dead.

Gordon Bostic

The Fourth Night

The fourth night Maryann collapsed
Appalled at what she'd seen.
He'd tried his best to shelter her
But fate would intervene.

The altercation was a shock
But staged for all to see.
The power they held over them
They'd execute with glee.

The woman did not have to die
But she had been provoked.
Until they got what they desired
And reaction invoked.

Her death they dared to orchestrate
Which proved they're all at risk
That provocations may increase
With challenges more brisk.

Day Five

They woke up to a thunderstorm
And thus, day five began.
With the weather no deterrent
To what had been the plan.

The elements would play no part
In forcing a delay.
And so, the Walk, itself, resumed
The same as yesterday.

But as they walked the storm grew worse
And they were soaked by rain.
Just then the hail began to fall
Where walking was a strain.

In the distance they heard sirens
That signaled an alarm.
The storm had grown much more intense
And threatened them with harm.

Although before they could react
The thing came into view.
A tornado bore down on them
With little they could do.

The guards had tried to rally them
To the side of the course.
But the winds had intensified
Where voices sounded hoarse.

The screams of those carried away
Were terrible to hear.
But he clung onto Maryann
While he was choked with fear.

The dying had cried out to God
In which he'd not believed.
He thought it was a fantasy
And all of them deceived.

Though when the storm had clearly passed
They had resumed the Walk.
Yet, all that they experienced
They never shared in talk.

Her Safety his Domain

He'd tried his best to shelter her
But the wind was too strong.
He lost his balance in a gust
That had shoved him along.

He fought as hard as he could fight
To get back to her side.
But found it near impossible
As it intensified.

He found that he'd grown terrified
Maryann may be harmed.
There were projectiles ev'rywhere
Which had made him alarmed.

He thought her safety his domain
But now he felt some doubt.
He'd thought her faith was placed in him
But to God she cried out.

The Walk Resumes

The guards proved to be relentless
To have the Walk resume.
They forced the walkers to their feet
Despite their sense of doom.

There clearly were some injuries
Though most were not severe.
There were a number who were lost
But concern was austere.

The few they found that could not walk
Had quickly been dispatched.
The act had been so commonplace
They all had grown detached.

The storm was not completely done
Though it was less intense.
They still must face the elements
To which they'd no defense.

A Noble Effort

When Truman came up next to him
It caught him by surprise.
For he thought that their agreement
Truman might compromise.

Though Truman had admired the fact
He chose her to protect
His mission's for the greater good
And that he should respect.

Truman said that it was noble
What he had vowed to do
But thought it was impractical
If to see the drive through.

The last thing Truman said to him,
"You can't save ev'ryone."
He turned to him with his reply,
"It starts by saving one."

Insidious

He found the Walk insidious
And flawed in its design.
There was no justice to be gained
Thus, none would they assign.

It's clear the public was misled
Believing this humane.
They'd not seen the degradation,
The suffering and pain.

Its purpose more than punishment
And order to maintain.
The malcontents, political,
That the Walk could contain.

For if there was an accident
There would be none to tell
The nature of the circumstance
Of how the walker fell.

The Evidence

In terms of physicality
He was stronger than her.
But Maryann had inner strength
He wished she could confer.

It came to her through her beliefs
And faith that she professed.
She seemed to have a guiding light
But had not been obsessed.

He asked her what had led her to
Believe what she believed.
He needed to see evidence
That it's not misconceived.

The evidence was in her heart
As that's where God resides.
Her faith, she said, was personal
And in her heart abides.

Not ev'rything can be explained,
She told him with a smile.
Her faith had slowly come to her
Although it took a while.

The Note

The note that Truman left for him
Truman hoped would explain
The only purpose to the Walk
Was cover to maintain.

There was a part of government
That few had been aware.
It existed in the shadows
Beyond the public's glare.

It functioned amid secrecy
And there were few who knew
The extent of its policies
Or what it'd dare to do.

It was his mission to expose
The danger it presents
But he feared it had discovered
The threat he represents.

The Sorrow that he Bore

She wished to pass the time of day
So, asked him of his wife.
Though the reaction she received
Revealed there was some strife.

The fact that she could not conceive
Had forced her to withdraw.
A child had been her one desire
No chance, the final straw.

She barely ever spoke to him
But when she did was brief.
As though a part of her had died
And she's possessed by grief.

Now his assignment to the Walk
May have pushed her away.
He feared that if he reached the end
He'd find she did not stay.

Gordon Bostic

The Evil that Consumes Men's Souls

The evil that consumes men's souls
Was clearly on display.
As no contrition had been shown
In what they'd do or say.

Guards demonstrated no regard
For life of any kind.
As they would shoot small animals
If any they should find.

Sometimes at night the guards would fight
For what was left behind.
Possessions of the ones who died
As if they're theirs to find.

He could not think of an excuse
The guards could ever give
Which could justify the treatment
That no one could forgive.

The Fifth Night

There were no rumors on night five
As all had been too tired.
Besides the Walk, there was the storm
And grief for those expired.

Exhaustion had its grip on them
And they're not halfway through.
The course had grown more difficult
Than, probably, was due.

It appeared Belmont a sadist
Who reveled in their pain.
Some guards began to postulate
That he may be insane.

Though tonight it's unimportant
As they're too tired to think.
For tomorrow brought more judgment
And all clung to the brink.

Day Six

On the sixth day they found bodies
Were strewn across the course.
A product of the storm they faced
And of the storm's true force.

The sight, itself, had seemed surreal
As though a graphic book.
Where even the ones most squeamish
Had found they're forced to look.

Though some had seemed as if asleep,
Some others ripped apart.
And Maryann had broken down
Which cut into his heart.

They weren't allowed to pause nor pray
For those who now were dead.
Their only focus was the Walk
And pushing on ahead.

Had Freedom been Achieved?

While the rumors had persisted
He just had not believed
That the storm provided cover
Where freedom some achieved.

The fact that Belmont had seemed calm
Would lend them no belief.
For if some walkers had escaped
They'd suffer no relief.

He thought the rumors were unfair
As purpose they're devoid.
The little hope that burned in them
Was now an empty void.

The rumors, though, would still persist
As they had entertained.
It's the only interaction
They socially maintained.

Gordon Bostic

A Change of Luck

He looked at Maryann and said
It seemed their luck had changed.
Despite the horror they'd been through
They had not been shortchanged.

She shook her head and smiled at him,
"It was not luck at all.
The Lord had shone his providence.
To think else was pure gall."

He marveled at her strength of faith
She wore as though a shield.
For all the terror they had faced
She had refused to yield.

She could not quantify her faith
But he knew it was real.
And it had seemed to bolster her
To add to her appeal.

The Vet's Demise

Quite often they would needle him
To see how he'd respond.
They thought the vet was damaged goods
And of him were not fond.

He followed orders to a tee
But was sullen and sad.
He'd cast aside indignities
Which made all the guards mad.

Because the vet would not react
To anything they tried.
They made his life a living hell
And food they had denied.

The vet died unexpectedly
As though he just gave up.
Though no one ever knew the cause.
There was no follow-up.

Gordon Bostic

The Price of Defiance

They'd randomly choose one to beat
Or physically harass.
The kid gloves had been put aside
And no one got a pass.

A guard had chosen Maryann
To be his latest foil.
Though when he had stood up to him
He saw the guard recoil.

Some nearby guards saw what occurred
And rallied to his aid.
They beat him soundly with batons
So for defiance paid.

They left him kneeling on the course
Guards thought to face his end.
But Maryann had come to him
Intending to defend.

Her fierceness caught them by surprise.
They meekly backed away.
Maryann helped him to his feet
And they were on their way.

Emotions were a Problem

Each day the goal was to survive
And walk that extra mile.
There was no cause to celebrate
Nor reason found to smile.

The repercussions had been harsh
And many made to cry.
For those guards thought responsible
Were clearly meant to die.

Their fear had slowly turned to hate
And vengeance some had swore.
If, somehow, they survived the Walk
Revenge they'd try to score.

But emotions proved a problem
They had realized too late.
They affected them physically
And played into their fate.

An Eclectic Group

They were a most eclectic group
That fate had chose to bind.
The criminals, the malcontents
And guards who proved unkind.

All thrown together in one place
To either sink or swim.
Where trust was like a chandelier
That quickly had grown dim.

All arranged in a hierarchy
To which they had been bound.
With the guards at the pinnacle
And malcontents the ground.

The criminals would catch a break
As they, guards understood.
The malcontents were ostracized
As guards found them no good.

Although that was mere perception.
The guards viewed both the same.
Despite the reason for the Walk
To them they're all fair game.

The Thirteenth Day

The thirteenth day the Walk would end
Or so Belmont had said.
Though no one knew if it was true
As most feared they'd be dead.

There was no reason to believe
The things they had been told.
For Belmont was a bit deranged
Whose heart was icy cold.

They had no clue what day it was
As time had lost meaning.
For the Walk claimed ev'ry moment
Unless they were sleeping.

The thirteenth day could be a year
For all that they had known.
As time was of no consequence
When you they'd clearly own.

They thought it was a fairly tale
Which few would ever see.
A refuge to be granted them
Where from this they'd be free.

Gordon Bastic

Rumors of Rape

There had been rumors there were rapes
As guards took liberties.
The female walkers were at risk
As they'd no guarantees.

He did not know if it was true
But he'd not take the chance.
He'd seen the things the guards would do
And saw them steal a glance.

He had made sure the guards had known
She'd not be easy prey.
Whatever plans they may have made
He'd make sure that they'd pay.

So, Maryann he had kept close
Under his watchful eye.
For he'd sworn he would protect her
Or in the effort die.

Scavengers

The guards were less than scavengers
Who preyed upon the weak.
And rumors had run rampant that
They'd kill to sneak a peek.

They would clamor over bodies
Of those who were dispatched.
All to rob them of the trinkets
To which they were attached.

And sometimes murders had occurred
When guards became like ghouls
Descending on the flashy ones
Who're unsuspecting fools.

There never was a reprimand
For what the guards would do.
As Belmont was the one in charge
And he would do it too.

Gordon Bostic

Her Strength

Though sworn to be her guardian
He found his one concern
There was a wisdom she possessed
He deeply wished to learn.

Though she knew fear like all the rest
A calm she seemed to show.
As though she made her peace with it
Should death she'd come to know.

Her faith she could not quantify
Though what she had believed
Had given her a sense of peace
That he'd never achieved.

He'd always seen a strength in her
That he could not profess.
And of that he'd grown envious
Which now he must confess.

The Sixth Night

The sixth night found them still in shock
From what they'd seen that day.
They never were a close knit group
But none should die that way.

Some walkers grew ill physic'ly
So ghastly was the sight.
Where those who tried to go to sleep
Found replays in the night.

He'd grown concerned for Maryann
As quiet she became.
She'd always been so positive
But tonight not the same.

Perhaps she had been traumatized
By what she had to face.
He only hoped she had not thought
That he, she must replace.

Gordon Bostic

Day Seven

Day seven they'd begun the climb
They all had come to dread.
For anyone that fell behind
Was just as good as dead.

The incline had been torturous
And, thus, their pace had slowed.
The climb had been quite arduous
Where weariness they showed.

It was clear some had given up
Accepting of their end.
They simply laid down on the course
For guards to soon ascend.

The gunshots became meaningless
In effort to survive.
As he and Maryann struggled
To walk and stay alive.

The Walk had grown more tedious
With ev'ry step they took.
Like zombies of apocalypse
Who shared a vacant look.

Questioning

He found guards standing over him
When they roused him from sleep.
They had some questions to be asked
Where answers would not keep.

It's Truman they had asked about
And what it was he knew.
Truman had claimed they're watching him
And now he knew it's true.

They held a gun on Maryann
As answers they required.
What interactions did he have
That Truman had inspired?

He replied he had met him once
While they were on the Walk.
They merely exchanged pleasantries
But did not really talk.

It seemed they were not satisfied
When they had turned to leave.
But he had felt such great relief
That he'd won a reprieve.

Gordon Bostic

She Never Flinched

She never flinched a single inch
Nor at the gun had stared.
As though she knew this day may come
And she had been prepared.

She was not confrontational
Certain that's a mistake.
The guards had proven all too well
Their lives they'd gladly take.

She trusted he knew what to do
So did not make a move.
She merely stood and stared towards them
That she did not approve.

The courage Maryann displayed
Had not been a surprise.
For he had seen enough of her
To know that she was wise.

Darker Days

Darker days were now upon them
He could not have foreseen.
For ev'rything that had occurred
Had seemed beyond pure mean.

Guards demonstrated no regard
For life of any kind.
As walkers cruelly were dispatched
With no mercy to find.

And Belmont gave new meaning to
The concept of the beast.
Their welfare was not his concern
As he'd not cared the least.

Though he could not be positive
He can't ignore the dread
From what they had experienced
What yet may lie ahead.

Gordon Bostic

A Guard was Killed

The rumors spread a guard was killed
Sometime within the night.
They had suspicions but no proof
Nor reason could they cite.

But it became quite obvious
The guards were now on edge.
They really weren't a pleasant group
But now had walked the ledge.

Without a shred of evidence
It's clear they had assumed
A walker was responsible
Which meant they all were doomed.

The harshness they experienced
Had only seemed to grow.
Until they found the guilty one
It's pain they all would know.

The number of abuses grew
Where limits knew no bound.
For a walker was responsible
That had not yet been found.

The Message

The body that was crucified
Was there for all to see.
It was meant to be a warning
There was no guarantee.

And all were forced to look at it
So that they could be sure
The message that was sent to them
Was one that would endure.

He tried to hide the shock he felt
When he had seen the face.
For it was Truman hanging there
Whose body they'd deface.

A sudden chill ran down his spine
For he was still alive.
Unconsciously, he cupped his hand
Around the small thumb drive.

Gordon Bostic

His Only Thoughts

The only thoughts that came to him
Had been those of his wife.
Though Maryann had grown on him
It's Beth who was his life.

Their life was built on dreams they shared
When first they had been wed.
But now, due to his circumstance
Those dreams were all but dead.

The Walk had filled him with regrets
For what she had been through.
Though he'd been called a criminal
Did not mean it was true.

Each step he took, he took for her
In struggle to survive.
So far he felt quite fortunate
That he was still alive.

The Seventh Night

That night they rested at the top
Preparing for descent.
He found that sleep was difficult
And time was not well spent.

But questions had raced through his mind
Depriving him of sleep.
Why did Truman give him the drive
And trusted him to keep?

He stroked the hair of Maryann
While she was fast asleep.
Whatever choice he had to make
His promise he would keep.

A bigger burden he now bore
All due to Truman's trust.
Whatever choice he had to make
Will be because he must.

Reassured

She told him that he must have faith
If they're to make it through.
The Lord, she said, watched over them
And he must know it's true.

What good is faith to one who's doomed
He cried out to the void.
Then fell upon his knees and cried
As hope he was devoid.

Sometimes a touch is all we need
To find that we're assured.
And so it was when she touched him
That he was reassured.

We find our faith when we have need
And not a sec before.
Their circumstance could not be worse
And he'd not take much more.

Day Eight

Day eight had marked the great descent
Where more would likely die.
The decline had been quite severe
So, none had dared to fly.

But gravity had been a threat
They all were well aware
That once momentum had been gained
The walkers should beware.

A woman right in front of them
Had tripped before she fell.
He knew he could not get to her
So, warning he would yell.

An old man she had rolled into
Went crashing to the ground.
It was clear that both were injured
But all just walked around.

Gordon Bostic

Not one had stopped to offer aid
As though invisible.
For like zombies on a mission
They'd grown despicable.

Now stripped of their humanity
Who're little more than beast.
Who'd slowly turned on one another
With souls that were deceased.

Each step he took marked him with shame
And filled his heart with doubt.
But when he thought he may go back
He heard two shots ring out.

The Interrogation

It's Belmont who had summoned him
Which caused his heart to race.
Interrogations would be made
As Satan he would face.

His guards had searched him head to toe
But nothing did they find.
It's clear they thought he had something
For which they clearly pined.

He heard Belmont's assurances
He need not be afraid.
Some information he desired
In which he wished his aid.

He told Belmont he had no clue
What aid he could provide.
His goal was to complete the Walk
And cast all else aside.

Belmont then looked him in the eye
And told him if he'd lie
The little girl that he protects
This day would surely die.

From the start it was obvious
Truman was his concern.
Whatever knowledge he possessed
Belmont had wished to learn.

Gordon Bostic

It seemed Belmont was serious.
Perhaps somewhat afraid.
There must be something Truman knew
That could not be relayed.

He said he met him on the Walk
And they had talked awhile.
But they'd had nothing in common
And lasted just a mile.

Belmont said he was satisfied
Though he was not that sure.
He knew that they'd be watching him
With intent that wasn't pure.

Annette's Death

He saw the guards surrounding her
But reason had not known.
Annette did nothing that he saw
Such action should be shown.

She thought that she was one of them
Which had been a mistake.
For clearly she'd been targeted
And would receive no break.

He heard her beg but they ignored
Her plea for leniency.
When next a guard had shown to her
No hint of decency.

She cried for help but no one dared
To rally to her aid.
For no one dared to intercede
As they were too afraid.

Her cries had slowly come to end
And, sadly, he knew why.
For like the others he just watched
As young Annette would die.

Gordon Bostic

Maryann had been Horrified

Maryann had been horrified
To see what she had seen.
It seemed the guards possessed no souls
Or what they had, obscene.

A guard slipped behind Miranda
Then shot her in the head.
And for no apparent reason
Miranda now was dead.

The guard had said she tried to run
But that had been a lie.
For all of them had seen the act
And cursed him for reply.

It seems our sins return to us
When we may least expect.
When Belmont heard what he had done
He killed the guard direct.

What Kind of God?

What kind of god would stand for this.
Supporting its endgame?
She said there had been only one
And He was not to blame.

For in His wisdom He gave man
The true gift of free will.
Then God had simply backed away
To see what He'd instill.

So, God is not responsible
For what mankind may do.
He may offer them His guidance
If they should ask Him to.

But, otherwise, it's up to man
To accept he's to blame.
For all the evil mankind does
Is only man's to claim.

Gordon Bostic

Jackson

There'd been no guiding principles
Only thoughts of revenge.
Annette had been a friend of his
He swore he would avenge.

After Belmont dispatched the guard
He merely turned to leave
When Jackson had confronted him
Without a chance to grieve.

He called Belmont a murderer
Who had lost all control.
His guards were mostly savages
Devoid of any soul.

Then Jackson took a swing at him
Though, sadly, he had missed.
While Belmont calmly pulled his gun
And Jackson was dismissed.

The Adversary

The adversary that he faced
He came to recognize
Had never been the Walk at all
But what he failed to prize.

It's only through his strength of will
A man can be defined.
Not by his status nor his wealth
Nor if he is refined.

Humiliation they bestowed
And stripped humanity
But one thing that they could not take
Had been his dignity.

For no man was ever broken
Unless he would allow
For the strength of his convictions
Be made to disavow.

Gordon Bostic

The Eighth Night

The eighth night Maryann confessed
She had a crush on him.
She knew it was impossible
But, truly, was no whim.

It came to him as a surprise
So he was unprepared.
It was not love he felt for her
Although for her he cared.

A situation unforeseen
Now stared him in the face.
His love had been reserved for Beth
And steps could not retrace.

He wished to gently let her down
But she already knew
The love that she had felt for him
He had not felt it too.

Day Nine

The ninth day brought provocation
As all had been on edge.
The more their desperation grew
The less that they could hedge.

There was a sense of hopelessness
And over them a pall.
A sense that death's a certainty
That was meant for them all.

Thus, provocations from the guards
Had not been well received.
A tinderbox awaited them
The guards had not conceived.

Belmont lacked the understanding
They could be pushed too far
And there had been a threshold
Beyond which they would spar.

Gordon Bostic

Temptation

He'd confess that he'd been tempted
And now he felt ashamed.
Though Maryann had turned her back
He felt he can't be blamed.

Perhaps it was his own despair
That let it get this far.
The signs were clearly there to see
And now may leave a scar.

There're tell-tale signs that he had missed
Or had been misapplied.
Perhaps a subtle message sent
He'd no wish to provide.

He knew there'd surely be a risk
To be her guardian,
For sometimes gratitude can turn
Someone to partisan.

He had not meant to lead her on
Or show in any way
That he would turn his back on Beth
And with her run away.

An Awkward Silence

While they walked in awkward silence
They both had felt regret.
For they both had expectations
That, so far, were not met.

For her, it's unrequited love.
For him, it's questioning.
She wished she'd never said a word
And he, tired of guessing.

They shared much more than either wished
Where secrets were no more.
And now an awkward silence fell
That neither would restore.

In awkward silence they had walked
As both had felt ashamed.
Too many passions were revealed
That, so far, went untamed.

Gordon Bostic

The Whispers

For two days they'd heard the whispers
A break was to be made.
No details had been passed along
Which had left him afraid.

A revolution was at hand
Of which he'd have no part.
He thought it would be suicide
The moment it should start.

For if a massive break occurred
It could be an excuse
To let the guards unleash on them
New levels of abuse.

He leaned to Maryann and said
That something was afoot.
Then solemnly he cautioned her
No matter what, stay put.

For if the rumor should be true
He feared the consequence.
As retribution was assured
And soon it would commence.

A Government that Prides Itself

A government that prides itself
Above the ones it serves
Becomes unworthy of respect
Nor loyalty deserves.

The one thing that the Walk reveled
There was a great divide.
He saw it as the Walk progressed
Across the countryside.

Sometimes a town they would pass through
Where they were met with cheers.
Sometimes a city they'd traverse
Where they were met with jeers.

It seemed the shadow policies
Began to take their tolls.
For with ev'rything it'd taken
It'd not claimed all their souls.

Gordon Bostic

Reactions

Ev'ry action breeds reaction
Or so he understood.
But here reactions weren't allowed
As they would prove no good.

For here reactions bred contempt
Where sharply they'd respond.
Where a reaction they'd not liked
They'd quietly abscond.

They'd provoke for a reaction
As that would give them cause
To unleash their sullen fury
Delivered without pause.

So, those surviving quickly learned
They never should react.
For death was what awaited them
And that was just a fact.

The Revolt

The revolt broke out suddenly
But had not been well planned.
Because the chaos that ensued
Proved they were undermanned.

The ones who made a break for it
Were instantly dispatched.
For clearly those in the revolt
Were greatly overmatched.

The guards in front were overwhelmed
For they had been surprised.
Their weapons they had forfeited
As they were greatly prized.

Gunfire was indiscriminate
Not caring who was killed.
There was no place where they could run
So, innocents had milled.

He used his body as a shield
To protect Maryann.
He knew that it was dangerous
But he'd no time to plan.

He heard the cries of those who're shot
But had not dared to look.
His focus was protecting her
No matter what that took.

Gordon Bostic

It seemed to be eternity
That all out war had raged.
Until the guards regained control
And the revolt assuaged.

When the revolt had been shutdown
The injured they'd inspect.
Where anyone who had been hurt
They viewed as circumspect.

Where any wounded who'd still breathe
No matter how they pled.
The guards regarded as a threat
And shot each in the head.

The Ninth Night

The ninth night she had need of him
As she had not before.
Today had been a tragedy
And she'd feared there'd be more.

The heartless cruelty on display
She just could not believe.
To see how they had murdered them
She just could not conceive.

She told him this must be a test
To see if her faith waned
In witness to insanity
From which they'd not abstained.

The Walk, so far, a travesty
Where lives they would condemn
And only through the grace of God
The guards had not killed them.

Gordon Bostic

Day Ten

The tenth day started with new rules
Which was Belmont's response
To what occurred the day before
Though spoke with nonchalance.

As Belmont felt they had to pay
For their lack of respect.
The Walk would be much harsher now
Than what they could expect.

The attempted coup cost him time
When he had none to spare.
So, any further disrespect
Would end in their despair.

At night they'd be allowed to rest
But only he would know
The length of time that they could sleep
Before they had to go.

Their rations would be cut in half
And gone were midday breaks.
Their pace of walk would be increased
No matter what it takes.

A Schedule to be Met

It was to be their midday break
That Belmont had denied.
Their progress had been pitiful
As if they had not tried.

There was a schedule to be met
And they'd fallen behind.
So, there would be no midday break
Nor breaks of any kind.

Their laziness had jeopardized
The promise Belmont made.
So ev'ry second that they'd lost
He ordered be repaid.

Whomever by the wayside fell
No blame was Belmont due.
There was a schedule to be met
But they'd not followed through.

Gordon Bostic

The Ones Who Came Before

The bloody footprints left a trail
Of those who came before.
The ones whose shoes had worn away
With feet blistered and sore.

The ones who struggled up ahead
To walk despite the pain.
For if they'd hesitate to walk
It's death they would obtain.

The ones who're blinded by the tears
Assured that death was near.
As their feet began to fail them
With pain replaced by fear.

The ones who fought the agony
Of taking one step more.
The ones knowing if they faltered
It's death they'd next explore.

They Had Their Own Agenda

Those deep within the government
Had each lived like a king.
Enjoying all the luxuries
That unjust taxes bring.

Though none had dared to question how
Their wealth had been obtained.
Suspicions had been numerous
That it was falsely gained.

Despite administrative change
These people still survive.
For they labored in the shadows
Where they're allowed to thrive.

They don't create the policies.
Their charge was to enforce.
Where they could take some liberties
And could chart their own course.

In the middle of the shadows
They'd scurry as if mice.
For they had their own agendas
They would not sacrifice.

Gordon Bostic

Brianne

There had been no indiscretions
To which Brie would admit.
But it was clear that some event
To which she would commit.

His promises were wasted breath
Which Brie had learned firsthand.
She'd become more than a walker
Subject to his command.

When there're no more indignities
She'd readily accept.
He passed her to a group of guards
Who took her while she wept.

They passed her body by the course
Where, clearly, she had died.
As though she was a piece of trash
That had been casted aside.

An Open Heart

He'd never tried to pray before
Because he'd not known how.
So, he had turned to Maryann
To ask her teach him now.

She said a prayer's not a wish
But guidance he should seek.
To place his faith where she placed hers
Accepting they're both weak.

And allow his heart to open
To what he knew was true.
For a heart that was not open
God can't enter into.

She said there were no guarantees
Despite how hard he'd pray.
Though there always was an answer.
Sometimes the answer's nay.

But she trusted in His judgment
For He knew more than she.
But admitted some frustration
In what she could not see.

Conflicted

He often thought he'd take a knee
And bring this to an end.
But then he thought of Maryann
Whom he'd sworn to defend.

But he had grown so tired of this
Death would be a release.
They'd put a bullet in his head
And, maybe, he'd find peace.

But Maryann he'd leave behind
As subject to her fate.
Perhaps her faith would pull her through
And danger she'd abate.

Though there were no assurances
She'd make it to the end.
So, he kept walking like a drone
To watch over his friend.

With Tensions Running High

Each day they'd grown more desperate
And as fatigue set in
The walkers grew more obstinate
Much to the guard's chagrin.

Thus, tensions had been running high
With courage a mistake.
As guards had been unhesitant
In choices they would make.

Any sign of provocation
Had spawned a harsh reply.
Where some were beaten half to death
And others left to die.

The Walk had been a travesty
Of cruelty and abuse.
And though the walkers had complained
It was of little use.

And ev'ryday saw tragedy
As more and more were killed.
While guards had merely reveled in
The blood that had been spilled.

Gordon Bostic

The Midnight Stroll

They could not see a single thing
As there had been no light.
Belmont decreed to make up time
They'd walk throughout the night.

The guards had found it humorous
How walkers tripped and fell.
For the guards possessed equipment
Where they could see quite well.

The darkness, though, brought some relief
At least it had been cool.
Although he felt his legs may fail
Due to a lack of fuel.

But darkness was a handicap
And thus, mistakes were made.
A walker wandered off the course
And with his life he paid.

Day Eleven

Day eleven an extension
What was the day before.
For they had walked throughout the night
And could not walk much more.

There was no mercy for the damned
As all were meant to die.
Although he knew if none survived
There would be questions why.

Yet, still he drove them well beyond
What most men could endure.
And those who failed to keep the pace
Had found a short tenure.

When, finally, he called a halt
Most walkers had collapsed.
They swore that Belmont lost his mind
Or conscience had elapsed.

They begged him for a longer rest
Which Belmont had ignored.
He had a schedule to maintain
And these he had deplored.

And those who found they could not rise
Had pleaded to be spared.
So heartless had the Walk become
No guard had even cared.

Gordon Bostic

Though many had wept openly
So dark was their despair.
Belmont had stood in overwatch
And clearly did not care.

The rest had been inadequate
And many could not rise.
The guards gave each one final chance
Then hastened their demise.

The Midday Sun

The midday sun beat down on them
Which made the Walk much worse.
It went beyond mere punishment
And bordered on a curse.

The gunshots now were meaningless
So often were they heard.
As exhaustion overcame
Where wish to live was blurred.

Where walkers had refused to walk
Or simply had collapsed.
As dehydration took its toll
And judgment greatly lapsed.

He held on tight to Maryann
To keep her on her feet.
As both of them were struggling
In the face of defeat.

When Belmont called for them to stop
They should have felt relief.
Instead they had been overcome
With a strong sense of grief.

Gordon Bostic

His Thoughts

His thoughts would often turn to Beth
For all he did was walk.
He wondered if she missed him now
As she'd refused to talk.

She'd never been the only one
That he had cared about.
But he had always stood by her
And to her was devout.

He wondered if she even cared
That he'd been forced away.
This gave her opportunity
To choose to leave or stay.

Now with all that he was facing
His thoughts would turn to her.
And although he tried to squelch them
The thoughts he can't defer.

A Sense of Faith (Reprise)

A sense of faith had come to him,
Perhaps, because of her.
She had a strength he did not have
That, somehow, she'd confer.

He wondered, though, this need for faith
Was due to circumstance.
Or had he grown so desperate
He'd dare to take the chance.

Perhaps he had a fear of faith
That's why he never prayed.
He'd not believed an unseen force
Could have a diff'rence made.

But Maryann convinced him that
Things greater than oneself
Had clearly been made evident
As he had seen himself.

Day Twelve

Day twelve they woke with new found hope
The Walk was almost done.
He was dismayed so few remained
Although he had been one.

They mostly were acquaintances
He'd not considered friends.
But few of them deserved the fate
That led them to their ends,

They stripped them of humanity
And made them feel debased.
By forcing them to live in filth
So that their sins were faced.

Though the justice system failed them
It had not failed them all.
For some deserved deliverance
And some deserved to fall.

The Walk was promise of reform
Or so they had been told.
But justice seemed to be a dish
That it had wished served cold.

The Government had been Appalled

The government had been appalled
So many still survived.
For Belmont's mission had been clear
To whom should be archived.

This group had been more dangerous
Than any group before.
Because the knowledge they possessed
Could strike it at its core.

The risk it took, already great,
To put them in one place.
But trusted that the circumstance
Could prevent face to face.

Then it left it up to Belmont
To do what must be done.
So, when the Walk had been complete
Those finishing were none.

Cleaning House

Because his orders were precise
Belmont had little choice.
He needed to start cleaning house
And keep to its invoice.

They only were one day away
From where the Walk would end.
And he still had some malcontents
With whom he must contend.

Their deaths could not be obvious
While this close to the end.
With the chance of some surveillance
And acts could not defend.

The twelfth night would present the chance
His orders to fulfill.
When all of those who're targeted
He silently would kill.

His Dreams

He had dreams of retribution
For all they had been through.
In answer for indignities
He felt they were not due.

He'd never been an angry man
But he was angry now.
Guards preyed on their frailties
As only they knew how.

He dreamed one day he'd have revenge
Where they would come to know
The terror he experienced
That they seemed to love so.

He'd never been a faithful man
But if he was to pray
It was vengeance he would ask for
To make these bastards pay.

Gordon Bastic

A Day of Reckoning

The anger that had welled in him
Had begged for its release.
He'd never been a forceful man
But that was soon to cease.

There'd be a day of reckoning
To that he made a pledge.
Where one day they'd be made to pay
For all the pain they'd dredge.

In life he'd known disappointment
And the meaning of sad.
But this had been quite different
As he was truly mad.

While faced with the atrocities
They were forced to endure
There'd be a day of reckoning
Of that he had been sure.

The Blackness of Abyss

She saw a subtle change in him
That only she could see.
Resentment had its hold in him
And he could not break free.

He'd been a good man all his life
But seemed under the strain
The goodness that had filled his heart
Began to slowly drain.

She felt the anger grow in him
With ev'ry life they took.
He'd never dared to speak of it
But she had seen the look.

She told him that he'd need true faith
So anger could dismiss.
Before his anger led him to
The blackness of abyss.

The Lord had saved him once or twice
Which he could not deny.
She told him it was crystal clear
He knew the reason why.

Gordon Bostic

A Need to Pray

He found he had a need to pray
As that's all he had left.
He found his courage faltering
And faith he was bereft.

He wanted to get home to Beth
But chances had looked slim.
For he felt some paranoia
That they would target him.

So many they'd already killed
He feared a fact of time
That payment he was due to pay
For what they called a crime.

He feared that he'd been targeted
As if they somehow knew
That Truman had appeared to him
With things they weren't to view.

The Twelfth Night

He saw the night as biblical
When justice would be served.
Where malcontents to government
Would get what they deserved.

An angel would descend on them
For as the walkers slept
It was the night of reckoning
As death among them crept.

His guards were eager to assist
As long as they got paid.
They had no qualms to what's required
By the decisions made.

For none of them were innocent
As country they betrayed.
Releasing info classified
And secrets they parlayed.

Now retribution was required
For acts that they'd performed.
These malcontents of government
Who never had conformed.

Gordon Bostic

A Loss of Hope

He felt the hope drain out of him
With each death that occurred.
The chance that any may survive
Had barely been inferred.

And it had been his assumption
They all were meant to die.
As though it's an imperative
Although he'd not known why.

Though they were mere acquaintances
He'd met along the way.
They each possessed the gift of life
Which guards had snatched away.

Each speck of hope would dissipate
With each shot that he heard.
He feared it's just a fact of time
Before he got the word.

A United Front

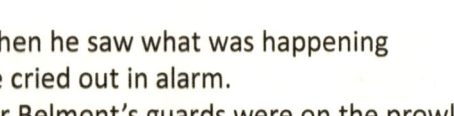

When he saw what was happening
He cried out in alarm.
For Belmont's guards were on the prowl
Intending to do harm.

A voice had caught him by surprise
That overcame his fear
And told him he must organize
For death was lurking near.

He begged the walkers to resume
The journey they began
For the course gave them protection
And ruined Belmont's plan.

He told the walkers to unite
And reform on the course.
For Belmont could not kill them all
So, he'd have no recourse.

The move caught Belmont by surprise
To see the Walk resume.
But this time voluntarily
And to avoid true doom.

While Belmont simply stood and stared
With plans which went awry.
They now showed a united front
Though he had not known why.

Gordon Bostic

A Leap of Faith

It truly was a leap of faith
But faith was all he had.
For ev'ry time he thought of her
It made him truly sad.

Although he lost her years ago
It seemed like yesterday.
His life had seemed so empty now
Since she'd pushed him away.

He prayed that he could help her heal
And grow to be less sad.
He knew it was a leap of faith
But that was all he had.

Undeniable

There had been questions that were raised
That swiftly were ignored.
For no one in the government
Had wished that path explored.

It had a fear of compromise
So, indications were
That any threat that it perceived
It quickly would deter.

Just based on moral principles
The Walk, it seemed, made sense.
For prison terms it felt too harsh
And not worth the expense.

Instead of having them confined
A penance they would pay.
Where they'd reflect on what they'd done
In some unpleasant way.

Yet, he'd come to have suspicions
The government had lied.
The Walk had been a testament
It would not be defied.

At first it had seemed ludicrous
The sentence that befell.
Their crimes were not that serious
To be condemned to hell.

Gordon Bostic

The criminals were camouflage
To hide its true intent.
Who, if by chance, should not survive
Would breed no true dissent.

He'd noticed as the Walk progressed
That of those who were slain
How few had been a criminal
Which was hard to explain.

It had been undeniable
To see what had been planned.
The Walk had simply been a ruse
Where malcontents were damned.

There was no justice to the Walk
Nor was there meant to be.
There're secrets that it would protect
With no uncertainty.

A Change of Heart

She told him all it took was faith
To ease his cares away.
She found it through experience
Each time she'd choose to pray.

Her words resounded in his heart
Because they seemed so true.
It's only by the grace of God
That they would make it through.

Maryann could be persuasive
When she turned on the charm.
There's nothing more he had to lose
So, he could see no harm.

He felt his anger dissipate
When he had bowed his head.
As though a weight had been removed
That sucked away his dread.

She always pointed to that night
When came his change of heart.
Although not yet a faithful man
That night had been the start.

Gordon Bostic

Awaiting Him

He wondered if he'd reach the end
Exactly what he'd find.
Would Beth be there awaiting him
Or she left him behind?

She was upset the day he left
Though it was not his choice.
He had so much he wished to say
But could not find his voice.

He worried if she's left alone
What choices she may make.
For she'd been inconsolable
And chances she may take.

So, all that's left is questioning
If, somehow, he'd return.
Would she be there awaiting him
Or he, she choose to spurn?

Day Thirteen

The thirteenth day should mark the end
For those who still remained.
The ones who'd shown a will to live
And wits had still retained.

The simple thought the Walk could end
Had made him want to cry.
To think that he survived it all
Against all those who'd die.

He found it hard to comprehend
With all that they'd been through.
The Walk was coming to an end
And freedom they were due.

The simple thought they had survived
Had been hard to believe.
Despite the perils they had faced
And threats that they'd receive.

Then Maryann he gave a hug
As though he had been crazed.
She smiled for him her brightest smile
Which he'd not seen for days.

Gordon Bostic

Newfound Hope

He saw grown men break down and cry
Believing they're home free.
They thought the end around the bend
To quash their misery.

There rose a sense of hopefulness
Since they were still alive.
The paltry few that still remained
And managed to survive.

The guards had laughed to see such joy
But had refused to say
The end the walkers thought was near
Was really miles away.

But bolstered by their newfound hope
The walkers upped their pace.
While no guard had the decency
To tell them not to race.

Rollercoaster

When Maryann had looked at him
He saw as no surprise
The feelings that she felt for him
She could help disguise.

With their journey near completion
There were some facts to face
The Rollercoaster that they rode
They never could retrace.

Though the words would go unspoken
They both knew gratitude.
For he had found a sense of faith
And she'd the Walk conclude.

And now the Walk was near complete
Both thought they'd put aside
The bevy of mixed emotions
That both tried hard to hide.

But the truth was unforgiving
Which he'd not seemed to see.
The love that she had felt for him
She never would be free.

Gordon Bostic

Belmont's Lament

Belmont stared in contemplation
As to the fact resigned
Some walkers made it to the end
Which had not been designed.

His orders had been very clear
And list it did provide.
But he had seemed untouchable
With each plan misapplied.

As though some force watched over him
Unfettered and unseen.
Where ev'ry plot that he devised
This mystic force would screen.

And because of this one failure
Some others had slipped through.
Which meant the shadow government
Would find it his miscue.

A Mended Heart

His absence seemed to mend Beth's heart
For she'd been left alone.
And in the silence she had found
What she had almost blown.

She blamed him where there was no fault
As reason she ignored.
While treatments were available
There're none she had explored.

She recognized there was a void
That he had seemed to fill.
For when they sent him to the Walk
Her life spiraled downhill.

In his absence she discovered
He meant much more to her
Than ever had been evident
Or fact she would defer.

Gordon Bostic

A Government in Shadows

A government built in shadows
Averts the people's will.
It only lives to serve itself
With its goals to fulfill.

Its only drive is its desires
And not the people's needs.
While it shows no hesitation
To make sure it succeeds.

Yet, because it hides in shadows
It's not held to account.
So, it will dare most anything
And laws it will surmount.

It denies its own existence
But claims the greater good.
It declares a noble calling
But was misunderstood.

The Finish Line

The finish line was just ahead
Which seemed to spark a race.
But the exertion took its toll
For those who broke their pace.

There're some whose legs simply gave out.
While others just collapsed.
Euphoria had taken them
And judgment clearly lapsed.

A crowd had gathered at the end
Of all the families.
All praying that their loved ones lived
Though had no guarantees.

He noticed he and Maryann
Also increased their pace.
It had been an unconscious choice
Although they did not race.

Then Maryann had just collapsed
Or, maybe, tripped and fell
But as she tried to right herself
Her knee began to swell.

Although she tried, she could not walk.
Her eyes reflected fear.
There was no way he'd leave her there
For she had been too dear.

The bloody footprints were his guide
As he could barely see.
For Maryann was in his arms
Due to an injured knee.

His total focus was the end
As he just stared ahead.
While he stepped across the bodies
Of those dying and dead.

He heard the cries of those gone lame
With the end in plain sight.
He had not dared to slow his pace
Though conscious of their plight.

He saw the end was just ahead
And he was almost there.
He heard the crowd begin to cheer
But he'd no longer care.

It's only through his strength of will
That had propelled him on.
Exhaustion had now dulled his mind
And reason was now gone.

His body had betrayed his mind
As he could barely think.
He felt as though he would collapse
Or teetered on the brink.

Each step he took he said a prayer
He could take one step more.
With his legs devoid of feeling
Each step had been a chore.

Each step he took could be his last
But now he had believed
The Lord was with him step for step
Till freedom he achieved.

He felt the hands grab hold of him
But could not fathom why.
They tried to rescue Maryann
Which he fought to deny.

But he had been too weak to fight
So, he lost Maryann.
Then he collapsed into a pile
When the blackout began

Gordon Bostic

Belmont's Address to the Crowd

Belmont had dared address the crowd
As worthy of their praise.
As though a hero had returned
Upon whom they now gazed.

Then Belmont claimed redemptive souls
Are what he had returned.
The ones he made to face their sins
And whose respect he'd earned.

Though his address had been drowned out
As grieving had grown loud.
There're few who even noticed him
'Cept curses from the crowd.

But Belmont was oblivious
To what the mood had been.
The media surrounded him
Whose story they would spin.

Regaining Consciousness

When, at last, he'd gained consciousness
The first thing he had seen
Was Beth was kneeling over him
Which was a welcomed scene.

He saw that tears ran down her cheek
Which, somehow, warmed his heart.
There're problems that they must address
But this could be a start.

He went to take her in his arms
But found that she recoiled.
For he'd become oblivious
To how bad he was soiled.

The only one who dared approach
Had offered him her hand.
She said her name was Brandywine
And thumb drive would demand.

Another one who did not care
It seemed was Maryann
Who limped to him and hugged him tight
To thank him while she can.

Gordon Bostic

The Hug

Beth thought the hug was held too long
Which caused her some concern.
She wondered what the Walk entailed
That this he'd come to earn.

She tried to ask him what occurred
But he refused to say.
Whatever happened on the Walk
He wished to lock away.

He saw her worry and concern
And said she should have none.
His love had never faltered once
As she's the only one.

For Maryann had watched his back
While he protected her.
It was a close relationship
But not who they now were.

But Beth had seemed unsatisfied
With how he had replied.
She wondered if he told the truth
Or cared so much he lied.

Justice would be Done

Although the shadows weren't dispersed
Some light they did restore.
For once their stories had been told
The Walk would be no more.

Though justice was its claim to fame
There's little they received.
They stripped them of their dignity
In ways they'd not conceived.

There was a lot of questioning
Plus, suspicions were raised.
Its purpose had been fallacy
Despite how it was praised.

The government had then declared
That justice would be done.
Whomever was responsible
Would have no chance to run.

Gordon Bostic

There Only Were Survivors

There'd been no cries of victory.
No celebrations made.
There had only been survivors
Whose debts in full were paid.

There'd been no wild hysteria
Nor any tears of joy.
There had only been survivors
Whose spirits they'd not buoy.

There'd been no gleeful repartee
Nor jokes of any kind.
There had only been survivors
With lives left undefined.

There had been no jubilation
Nor hints of any fame.
There had only been survivors
Who'd never be the same.

The Crowd

Though disappointment gripped the crowd
To see how few returned.
Caused the crowd to turn unruly
As anger in them burned.

The crowd descended on the guards
Where a melee ensued.
Police were called to intercede
Whom onlookers had booed.

The crowd held them accountable
For all that had occurred.
Some walkers even joined the crowd
For what they had endured.

Although when order was restored
The mood had never changed.
The crowd believed the Walk was cursed
And authors were deranged.

The Guard's Arrest

The guards were taken by surprise
When placed under arrest.
The walkers in proximity
Were vocal in unrest.

They did what they were ordered to
Was what they all had claimed.
It's Belmont who's responsible
And he who should be blamed.

Resisting his authority
Was one sure way to die.
Whatever orders Belmont gave
There was no asking why.

But as they each were led away
They cried it made no sense.
They're employed by the government
Had been their lone defense.

In His Absence

In his absence she discovered
What now she may have lost.
She'd felt her body was betrayed
But he she would accost.

She feared she'd disappointed him
As she was incomplete.
Should he find another woman
She feared she can't compete.

And now here comes this Maryann
And Beth could read the signs.
For there'd been infatuation
As on him she'd designs.

She could not blame him if he left
For it would be her fault.
She made his life a living hell
And heart she would assault.

Beth thought, perhaps, it was too late
And damage had been done.
With Maryann he'd gone through hell
And heart she may have won.

Gordon Bostic

His Demons

Every man has his demons
That he cannot be rid.
The secret lies he tells himself
Of things that he wished hid.

But Beth noticed that his demons
Had taken hold of him.
Where once his heart was light and gay
He now appeared so grim.

As though he had gained a burden
Somewhere along the Walk.
Or discovered newfound knowledge
Of which he would not talk.

She prodded and she poked at him
To get him to reveal
The depth of the experience
He tried hard to conceal.

Till, at last, he had relented
And agreed to bare all.
But told her to prepare herself
For what he could recall.

He really had no wish to die
But death had seemed assured.
He thought that he was targeted
When something else occurred.

A calming voice had come to him
To warn him of his plight.
For Belmont had a plan in place
Where he'd be killed that night.

But the warning had allowed him
To escape Belmont's plan.
Which then led him to the finish
Along with Maryann.

He thought it was the voice of God.
For that's what he believed.
The only reason he's alive
Was God's grace he received.

When he looked up, he had been shocked.
Completely unprepared.
For Beth was sitting mouth agape
While at him merely stared.

Gordon Bostic

Belmont's Confession

The night they took Belmont away
Belmont brushed next to him
And whispered that he had survived
When chances had been slim.

His name was on the target list
With one major concern.
If something bad happened to him
He feared the rest would turn.

The twelfth night he was meant to die
But fate would intervene
When he had noticed the attempt
And stirred up quite the scene.

He had been right when he declared
The facts that he'd discerned.
Too many questions would be asked
If none of them returned.

So, in a way he beat the odds
And fate he was assigned.
Which Belmont thought a miracle
Some unseen force designed.

The Shadows

The shadows were not ever purged
As they were too ingrained.
Its actions had been disavowed
But never were explained.

Some crimes had been so frivolous
He could not understand
Why they were sentenced to the Walk
And thus, like him were damned.

They say that justice should be blind
But he'd not found it so.
Because the bodies he had seen
Were those he'd come to know.

The shadows had proved dangerous
Beyond its policies.
The Walk was meant to cover-up
All its conspiracies.

Gordon Bostic

An Apology

Beth saw him staring into space
And sat down next to him.
She asked him what was on his mind.
He said it had been them.

For all the things that they'd been through
And what they'd yet to face.
He wondered if she trusted what
He said had taken place.

She said, of course, she trusted him
That had been no issue.
But found it hard to comprehend
All that he had been through.

Perhaps forgiveness he could find
If she would bare her heart.
And maybe an apology
Would be where she should start.

The Long Shower

The longest shower of his life
Was what had been required
To bring him back to normalcy
With cleanliness acquired.

He had not been completely dry
When Beth ran up to him.
She held him in a tight embrace
Where he'd not moved a limb.

She told him she had been a fool
For what she's put him through.
She thought about it quite a lot
While he was out of view.

He spoke of his discovery
As faith he had acquired.
Whatever problems they may face
They'd pray to be inspired.

And Maryann the reason why
As she the road had paved.
He thought he was protecting her
But he's who had been saved.

Gordon Bostic

The Thirteenth Night

The thirteenth night he laid in bed
And held Beth close to him.
Relieved that he survived the Walk
Though chances had been slim.

The Walk had cost him ev'rything
Or so it had appeared.
It forced him to leave Beth behind
And job had disappeared.

His parents fell to their despair
In how he had been tried.
And then within a day or two
Both of his parents died.

The horrors he experienced
Still haunted him at night.
Though Beth had now been there for him
To try to make things right.

The doctors said recovery
Would take a little time.
He should be grateful he survived
And pardoned for his crime.

But there was a silver lining
For two things he had found.
His faith was a discovery
And Beth had come around.

Belmont's Trial

He stood before the magistrate
Defiant of the charge.
For he was of the government
And should be left at-large.

The charges were ridiculous
Or so his lawyers claimed.
Whatever on the Walk occurred
He surely can't be blamed.

But witness after witness spoke
Of the atrocities.
With Belmont at the heart of it
At varying degrees.

The jury was not out for long
With verdict no surprise.
They found him guilty on all counts
And called for his demise.

Gordon Bostic

The Big Mistake

The courtroom seemed to overflow
The crowd had been so large.
Most praying justice would be served
And he's not left at-large.

They both attended Belmont's trial
But when there was a break
The both admitted to themselves
They'd made a big mistake.

It revived troubled memories
That he'd wished to forget.
He found no purpose had been served
And only made him fret.

The Walk had been a travesty
Which now most people knew.
So many people had been killed
Where death had not been due.

There was no wisdom that was gained.
No goal had been achieved.
The people sold a bill of goods
And found they were deceived.

The horrors they experienced
Were clearly a mistake.
But in the end and truth be told
No diff'rence did it make.

The Miracle

Each Sunday they attended church
As though a debt was owed.
But only Beth and he had known
It's gratitude they showed.

For clearly God watched over him
Throughout the sordid Walk.
And after all the things he'd seen
Of which he would not talk.

He relished Beth had come to find
The faith he'd grown to know.
It strengthened their relationship
And spurred their love to grow.

Perhaps it was their strength of faith,
As both of them believed.
That spawned what was a miracle.
The day that Beth conceived.

Gordon Bostic

Belmont's Fate

When Belmont had been brought to trial
He thought he'd be absolved.
As he worked for the government
And it, too, was involved.

He followed orders he received
Exactly as were charged.
So how was he accountable
For orders he discharged?

The DA brought in witnesses
That numbered near a score.
Who spoke of his atrocities
And to which they all swore.

The hangman's noose awaited him
And yet he'd still believe
That through the ones he was aligned
A pardon he'd receive.

Though when the platform was released
The last thought that he had
Those in the shadow government
Must really have been mad.

He Prayed the Evil Died

He prayed the evil died with him
But knew it was not true.
As he found no explanation
For evil that men do.

He hoped with Belmont dead and gone
His nightmares soon would end.
The memories he tried suppress
Would sometimes still ascend.

He feared the scars would never heal
Yet, faith he came to trust
He'd grow to be a better man
Because he felt he must.

The media reported it
But he had not believed
How numerous the suicides
Now freedom was achieved.

Gordon Bostic

The Task

While Beth was nursing their new son
She turned to him to ask
Why had he taken such a risk
In taking on the task?

He looked at her in puzzlement
Not sure of what she meant.
What task was she referring to
That led her to comment?

Why was it he'd accept the risk
And Maryann protect?
Someone he'd never met before
And may have been suspect.

It's true he feared he'd be betrayed
But even if that's true.
No other choice could he have made
But help her see it through.

Beth beamed a little smile at him
But nothing did she say.
He was a man of principle
She'd not let get away.

The Gathering

The walkers gathered one last time
To make a solemn vow.
Agreeing to meet once a year
And Walk to disavow.

When people face adversity
They tend to somehow bond.
Presented with a common threat
Together they respond.

No death would go unrecognized
Except, perhaps, a few
Whose sentence was legitimate
And earned what they were due.

So once a year they'd reunite
To mourn who had been lost.
Recalling the adversity
Of those who were star-crossed.

Then Maryann and he would meet
Though rarely would they talk
Of anything that's relevant
That had concerned the Walk.

Gordon Bostic

Brandywine

The government had come for him
To find out what he knew.
It seemed Brandywine was missing
As was the thumb drive, too.

He'd only met her the one time
While he was half aware
Of what it was she wished of him
That she would meet him there.

She claimed the drive held evidence
The government had lied.
And swore she would release the facts
To make sure all were tried.

There had been snippets she released
Through social media.
Which had led to speculation
Of wild hysteria.

Then rumors came they found her hung
And ruled it suicide.
The drive, it seemed, had disappeared
Or hidden 'fore she died.

Then a new Walk had been scheduled
To take place in a year.
For there was justice to be served
The government made clear.

About the Author

Gordon Bostic was born in West Virginia and grew up in Virginia. A graduate of James Madison University and Fairleigh Dickinson University, he worked as a computer scientist and a software engineer for most of his life. He began writing at a young age as a way of expressing himself, his feelings and his view of the world. Gordon has also had an interest in telling his stories in one way or another. "The Walk" is his sixth novel. Gordon currently lives on the Jersey Shore with his wife, Susan.